W9-BST-181

America

kneels to pray

America

kneels to pray

thirty-one days of prayer for our nation

Copyright ©2003 Elm Hill Books, an imprint of J. Countryman®, a division of Thomas Nelson, Inc.
Nashville, TN 37214

All rights reserved. No part of this book may be reproduced, stored in a retrieval system, or transmitted in any form or by any means—electronic, mechanical, photocopying, recording, or any other—except for brief quotations in printed reviews, without prior written permission of the publisher.

The quoted ideas expressed in this book (but not scripture verses) are not, in all cases, exact quotations, as some have been edited for clarity and brevity. In all cases, the author has attempted to maintain the speaker's original intent. In some cases, quoted material for this book was obtained from secondary sources, primarily print media. While every effort was made to ensure the accuracy of these sources, the accuracy cannot be guaranteed. For additions, deletions, corrections or clarifications in future editions of this text, please write ELM HILL BOOKS.

Scripture quotations are taken from:

The Holy Bible, New International Version (NIV) Copyright © 1973, 1978, 1984, by International Bible Society. Used by permission of Zondervan Publishing House. All rights reserved.

The Holy Bible, New King James Version (NKJV) Copyright © 1982 by Thomas Nelson, Inc. Used by permission.

The Holy Bible, New Living Translation (NLT) Copyright © 1996. Used by permission of Tyndale House Publishers, Incorporated, Wheaton, Illinois 60189. All rights reserved.

The New American Standard Bible®, (NASB) Copyright © 1960, 1962, 1963, 1968, 1971, 1972, 1973, 1975, 1977, 1995 by The Lockman Foundation. Used by permission.

Cover Design by Denise Rosser
Page Layout by Bart Dawson

ISBN 1-4041-8442-2

Printed in the United States of America

table of contents

America prays...

America prays...

introduction

The events of September 11, 2001 demonstrated all too clearly that we live in a dangerous world. Previously, Americans could take comfort in the fact that our homes were protected, at least in part, by two vast oceans. No longer. Today, we face a new reality: the threats to our nation are far different and far more immediate than those encountered by our forebears. Yet, we are no different from earlier generations in one profound respect: we still need God. Americans still turn to God for guidance, for strength, for comfort, and for love.

Abraham Lincoln spoke for countless believers when he confessed, "I have been driven many times to my knees by the overwhelming conviction that I had nowhere else to go." As concerned citizens, we know how Mr. Lincoln must have felt. The complexities of our world require vision beyond the capability of any single man or woman, no matter how wise. How, then, can we survive? A.W. Tozer directs us to the answer: "Leadership requires vision, and whence will vision come except from hours spent in the presence of God in humble and fervent prayer?" In other words, if we are to survive and prosper in a difficult world, we must turn our thoughts and our prayers to God.

Today, America desperately needs our prayers. Our troops are stationed in distant lands; the world in which we live is a perilous place; and the forces that seek to destroy us are as determined as they are fanatical. All across the globe, brave men and women continue to offer the ultimate sacrifice in order to protect the liberties that we hold dear. But we, too, must do our part to preserve freedom. And so it is that we—as God-fearing and God-trusting Americans—must follow the lead of Abraham Lincoln: we must drop to our knees in prayer.

☆

12

☆

This text is designed to assist readers in a 31-day prayer vigil for our nation. For a month, readers are asked to consider the thoughts on these pages and then to pray for the needs of our country. God's Word directs our nation to seek Him and to pray; His Word commands us to turn away from evil and to seek His will. When we do, God guides our paths.

America is strong because Americans have been, and continue to be, a praying people. Now, more than ever, we must exercise our God-given responsibility: the privilege of sincere, heart-felt prayer.

1

America prays...
for Our Nation

Then if my people who are called by my name
will humble themselves and pray and seek
my face and turn from their wicked ways,
I will hear from heaven and will forgive
their sins and heal their land.

2 Chronicles 7:14 NLT

"One nation, under God . . . ." We have heard these words so often that we sometimes take them for granted. After all, God has richly blessed America throughout its history. And why, we ask, would He not continue to bless us? But we must beware: to take God's blessings for granted is to deny Him the praise and glory that He both deserves *and* commands.

Because America is a land of religious freedom and tolerance, it has become a melting pot, not only of people, but also of faiths. We Americans are free to worship God as we see fit. But worship Him we must. Otherwise, we will stray from God's will and, in doing so, put ourselves—and our nation—in grave danger.

Today and every day, may we praise God through our words and our deeds, both as individuals and as a nation. When we do, we will surely remain one nation, blessed beyond measure, and watched over by a loving and merciful God.

☆
16
☆

The sacred writings tell us that
"except the Lord builds the House,
they labor in vain that build it." I therefore
beg that henceforth prayers imploring the
assistance of heaven, and its blessings on our
deliberations, will be held in this Assembly
every morning before we proceed to business.
Ben Franklin
(Philadelphia Constitutional Convention, 1787)

☆
17
☆

I have found the perfect antidote for fear.
Whenever it sticks up its ugly face,
I clobber it with prayer.
Dale Evans Rogers

Do not pray for easy lives.
Pray to be stronger men.
John F. Kennedy

A Prayer for America

Heavenly Father, America is my home, a land
that You have blessed beyond measure. You
have poured out your blessings on this nation,
Lord; let me praise You for Your glorious
works. Today, I pray for America; I pray that
this nation might follow Your Word and Your
will. Make this nation a land of righteousness,
courage, compassion, and love for You.
Amen

☆
18
☆

2

America prays...
for Those Who Serve

The greatest among you must be a servant.
But those who exalt themselves will be
humbled, and those who humble
themselves will be exalted.
Matthew 23:11-12 NLT

The future of our nation depends, in large part, upon the sacrifices made by those who serve and protect us. Let us pray for these brave men and women.

Jesus made it clear: We achieve greatness through service to others. But, as weak human beings, we sometimes fall short as we seek to ☆ puff ourselves up and glorify our own 20 accomplishments. And sometimes, we fail to do ☆ our part to serve others. Jesus commands otherwise. If we seek spiritual greatness, we must first become servants.

Today, our nation needs our prayers *and* our service. May we, as Christians, offer both. Let us begin by offering our prayers to God, and then, let us work courageously to fulfill His kingdom's work here on earth.

And so, my fellow Americans,
ask not what your country can do for you—
ask what you can do for your country.
John F. Kennedy

When you help your neighbors,
you help your nation.
Everybody can do something.
George W. Bush

☆
21
☆

Everybody can be great because
anybody can serve.
Martin Luther King, Jr.

Some people give time, some give money,
some their skills and connections,
some literally give their life's blood.
But everyone has something to give.
Barbara Bush

A Prayer for America

Dear Lord, I pray for those who serve our
nation. Guide them, Father, and protect them.
And create in me a servant's heart.
Let me follow in the footsteps of Your Son
Jesus who taught us by example that to be
great in Your eyes, Lord, is to serve others
humbly, faithfully, and lovingly.
Amen

☆
22
☆

3

America prays...
for Our Leaders

Obey your leaders and submit to their
authority. They keep watch over you
as men who must give an account.
Hebrews 13:17 NIV

In his first letter to Timothy, Paul writes, "I urge, then, first of all, that requests, prayers, intercession and thanksgiving be made for everyone—for kings and all those in authority, that we may live peaceful and quiet lives in all godliness and holiness" (2:1-2 NIV). Paul's advice still applies; we must pray for everyone, including our leaders.

☆
24
☆

This generation of Americans faces problems that defy easy solutions, yet face them we must. We need leaders whose vision is clear and whose intentions are pure. Daniel writes, "Those who are wise will shine like the brightness of the heavens, and those who lead many to righteousness, like the stars for ever and ever" (*12:3 NIV*). Let us pray that our leaders will walk in wisdom as they direct us along the paths of righteousness.

It takes leaders with vision to help
people with dreams.
Hubert H. Humphrey

We need to learn to set our course by the stars
and not by the lights of every passing ship.
Omar Bradley

You can never separate a leader's actions
from his character.
John Maxwell

Leadership is a combination of strategy
and character. If you must be without one,
be without the strategy.
Norman Schwarzkopf

A Prayer for America

Heavenly Father, I pray for those who
lead our country. Give them wisdom, courage,
compassion, and faith. Today, I lift up those to
whom You have entrusted the authority over
this great nation. May they turn to You for
guidance and for strength in all that they do.
Amen

☆
26
☆

4

America prays...
for Those Who Mourn

Blessed are those who mourn,
for they shall be comforted.
Matthew 5:4 NKJV

Grief is the price that life periodically extracts from those who live long and love deeply. When any of us experience a profound loss, darkness overwhelms us for a while, and it seems as if we cannot summon the strength to face another day—but, with God's help, we can. During times of heartache, we can turn to God, first for solace and then for renewal. When we do, He comforts us and, in time, He heals us.

Both as individual citizens and as a nation, we Americans mourn the loss of those who have paid the ultimate price for the freedoms we enjoy. Let us we pray for their families. And, let us all seek the healing hand of our loving Father so that we might feel His comfort and His peace.

☆
28
☆

We cannot always understand the ways of
Almighty God—the crosses which He
sends us, the sacrifices which He demands
of us. But, if we accept with faith and
resignation His holy will—with no looking
back to what might have been—
we are at peace.
Rose Fitzgerald Kennedy

He who becomes a brother to the bruised,
a doctor to the despairing, and a comforter to
the crushed may not actually say much. What
he has to offer is often beyond the power of
speech to convey. But the weary sense it,
and it is a balm of Gilead to their souls.
Vance Havner

☆
29
☆

The grace of God is sufficient for all our
needs, for every problem and for every
difficulty, for every broken heart,
and for every human sorrow.
Peter Marshall

A Prayer for America

Lord, You have promised that You
will not give us more than we can bear;
You have promised to lift us out of our grief
and despair; You have promised to restore our
souls. Today, Lord, I pray for those who mourn,
and I thank You for sustaining all of us in
our days of sorrow. May we trust You always
and praise You forever.
Amen

☆
30
☆

5

America prays...
for Peace

God has called us to peace.
1 Corinthians 7:15 NKJV

As a nation, we seek peace—but not peace at all costs. When America is threatened, we must defend her or risk losing the liberties that we hold dear. Yet, even when we struggle against forces that would destroy us, we pray for the ultimate victory: lasting peace.

The beautiful words of John 14:27 give us hope: "Peace I leave with you, My peace I give unto you . . . ." We, as believers, can accept God's peace or ignore it. When we invite the peace of God's into our lives, we are transformed. And then, because we possess the gift of peace, we can share that gift with fellow believers and with fellow citizens of all faiths.

Today, as a gift to yourself, to your family, to your friends, and to your nation, pray for peace in the world and for peace within your soul. Then, claim the inner peace that is your spiritual birthright: the peace that God intends for your life. It is offered freely; it has been paid for in full; it is yours for the asking. So ask. And then share.

☆
32
☆

Peace with all the world is my sincere wish.
I am sure it is our true policy, and
I am persuaded it is the ardent desire
of the government.
George Washington

Peace and friendship with all mankind
is our wisest policy, and I wish we may be
permitted to pursue it.
Thomas Jefferson

☆
33
☆

A great many people are trying to make peace,
but that has already been done.
God has not left it for us to do;
all we have to do is to enter into it.
D. L. Moody

God loves you and wants you to experience
peace and life—abundant and eternal.
Billy Graham

A Prayer for America

Dear Lord, You offer a peace that is perfect
and eternal. Let me turn the cares and burdens
of my life over to You, and let me feel
the spiritual abundance that You offer through
the person of Your Son, the Prince of Peace.
Today, I also pray for peace among nations,
Father, and for brotherly love among Your
children throughout the world. You are
the source of peace, Dear Lord;
let us find it in You.
Amen

☆
34
☆

6

America prays…
for God's Guidance

We can make our plans, but
the LORD determines our steps.
Proverbs 16:9 NLT

God has plans for America, but He won't force Americans to follow His will. To the contrary, He has given us free will, both as individuals and as a people. And, of course, with the freedom to choose comes the responsibility of living with the consequences of the choices we make.

Let us, as standard-bearers of the American Dream, seek guidance through the study of God's Word, and let us be watchful for His signs. God has richly blessed our nation, and He intends to use our nation in wonderful, unexpected ways. May we discover God's plan for our land, and may we follow it.

☆
36
☆

We have ample evidence that the Lord is able
to guide. The promises cover every imaginable
situation. All we need to do is to take
the hand He stretches out.

Elisabeth Elliot

When we entrust our requests to Him,
we trust him to honor our prayers
with holy judgment.

Max Lucado

He knows when we go into the storm,
He watches over us in the storm, and
He can bring us out of the storm when
His purposes have been fulfilled.

Warren Wiersbe

God uses ordinary people who are obedient
to Him to do extraordinary things.

John Maxwell

A Prayer for America

Dear Lord, I am Your creation, and
You created me for a reason. Give me the
wisdom to follow Your direction for my life's
journey, and give our leaders the wisdom
to direct our nation according to Your infinite
wisdom and Your perfect will. Lead us,
Father, and let us trust You completely,
today and forever.
Amen

☆
38
☆

7

America prays…
for God's Blessings

I will make you a great nation; I will bless you
and make your name great; and you shall be
a blessing. I will bless those who bless you,
and I will curse him who curses you;
and in you all the families of
the earth shall be blessed.

Genesis 12:2-3 NKJV

If we were to begin counting the blessings that God has bestowed upon our nation, the list would be improbably long. At the top of that list, of course, is the priceless gift of freedom: the freedom to live, to vote, to work, and to worship without fear. God has also blessed America with unsurpassed material wealth; we are, in fact, the most prosperous nation in the history of humanity.

As believers, we must never take God's blessings for granted. Instead, we must give thanks to the Giver for the many gifts that He has given us.

To those to whom much is given, much is expected, and so it is with America. We are the world's superpower, and as such, we have profound responsibilities to our own citizens and, to a lesser extent, to those who live beyond our borders. Our challenges are great, and no single individual, no matter how wise, can chart the proper course for our nation. But, *we the people*— under God and respectful of His command-ments—*can* join together to protect and preserve our nation and, in doing so, give protection and hope to freedom-loving people around the globe.

☆
40
☆

A mighty fortress is our God,
a bulwark never failing.
Martin Luther

The God who gave us life
gave us liberty at the same time.
Thomas Jefferson

God is the One who provides our strength,
not only to cope with the demands of the day,
but also to rise above them. May we look to
Him for the strength to soar.
Jim Gallery

God is more anxious to bestow His blessings
on us than we are to receive them.
St. Augustine

A Prayer for America

Lord, You have given me so much,
and I am thankful. Today, I seek Your
continued blessings for my life, for my family,
and for my nation. Let me share Your gifts with
others, and let my nation show generosity to
people throughout the world. We are blessed
that we might bless others. Let us give thanks
for Your gifts . . . and let us share them.
Amen

☆
42
☆

8

America prays…
for Those Who Suffer Around the World

Weeping may endure for a night,
but joy comes in the morning.
Psalm 30:5 NKJV

As Americans, we are fortunate to live in a land of opportunities and possibilities. But, for many people around the world, opportunities are scarce at best. In too many corners of the globe, hardworking men and women struggle mightily to provide food and shelter for their families.

The man from Galilee advised His followers, "I say to you, inasmuch as you did it to one of the least of these My brethren, you did it to Me" (Matthew 25:40 NIV). Jesus' words still apply.

When we care for the downtrodden, we follow in the footsteps of Christ. And, when we show compassion for those who suffer, we abide by the commandments of the One who created us. May we Americans hear the Word of God . . . and may we follow it.

Although the world is full of suffering,
it is also full of overcoming it.
Helen Keller

We must build a new world, a far better world,
one in which the eternal dignity
of man is respected.
Harry S Truman

☆
45
☆

To those peoples in the huts and villages
across the globe struggling to break the bonds
of mass misery, we pledge our best efforts to
help them to help themselves.
John F. Kennedy

It is the duty of every Christian
to be Christ to his neighbor.
Martin Luther

A Prayer for America

Heavenly Father, keep me mindful that
every man and woman, every boy and girl is
Your child. Let me give to the needy, let me
pray for those who mourn, and let me care for
those who suffer. And Father, let this great
nation be a symbol of generosity and caring to
needy people throughout the world.
Amen

☆
46
☆

9

America prays...
for Righteous Hearts

Blessed are those who hunger and thirst for
righteousness, for they shall be filled.
Matthew 5:6 NKJV

Because the Bible is God's guide for righteousness and salvation, it is unlike any other book. It contains thorough instructions which, if followed, lead to fulfillment, righteousness and joy. But if we choose to ignore God's commandments, either as individuals or as a nation, the results are as predictable as they are tragic.

☆
48
☆

A righteous life has many components: faith, honesty, generosity, love, kindness, humility, gratitude, and worship, to name but a few. If we seek to receive the blessings that the Father intends for our lives and four our country, we must live righteously and according to the principles contained in God's Holy Word. And, for further instructions, read the manual.

Let us have faith that right makes might,
and in that faith, let us dare to do
our duty as we understand it.
Abraham Lincoln

What is God looking for?
He is looking for men and women
whose hearts are completely His.
Charles Swindoll

☆
49
☆

If we have the true love of God in our hearts,
we will show it in our lives. We will not have
to go up and down the earth proclaiming it.
We will show it in everything we say or do.
D. L. Moody

Our progress in holiness depends on God
and ourselves—on God's grace and
on our will to be holy.
Mother Teresa

A Prayer for America

Lord, I pray that America might remain a
righteous nation, and I pray that I, too, might
live according to Your commandments.
When I take my eye away from You and Your
Word, I suffer. But, when I turn my thoughts,
my faith, my trust, and my prayers to You,
Heavenly Father, You guide my path.
Let me live righteously according to
Your commandments, and let me discover
Your will and follow Your Word
this day and always.
Amen

☆
50
☆

10

A Prayer for...
Strength in Times of Adversity

God is our refuge and strength,
a very present help in trouble.
Psalm 46:1 NKJV

The American dream was forged on the anvil of adversity. Tough times are nothing new to the American people: we've began facing and overcoming adversity long before John Hancock proudly penned his name on the Declaration of Independence. Through wars, epidemics, social unrest, and economic distress, Americans have faced their problems and risen above them. And so it is today. But through adversity, we grow stronger. Abigail Adams, said it well, "It is not in the still calm of life, or in repose of pacific station that great characters are formed...Great necessities call our great virtues."

The times that try men's souls are also the times when wise men and women to turn to God in prayer. E.M. Bounds writes, "God shapes the world by prayer. The more praying there is in the world, the better the world will be, and the mightier will be the forces against evil." Today, as in years gone by, America will grow stronger as we turn to the Creator of the universe for the victory that only He can provide.

☆
52
☆

It is part of the American character to consider nothing as desperate, to surmount every difficulty by resolution and contrivance.

Thomas Jefferson

Down through the centuries, in times of trouble and trial, God has brought courage to the hearts of those who love Him. The Bible is filled with assurances of God's help and comfort in every kind of trouble which might cause fears to arise in the human heart. You can look ahead with promise, hope, and joy.

Billy Graham

☆
53
☆

Christians are like tea bags.
It's only when they get into hot water that you find out how strong they are.

Anonymous

A Prayer for America

Lord, we give You thanks in all circumstances.
And, when we face the inevitable challenges
and difficulties of life, we turn to You.
When we encounter situations that we cannot
understand, we trust in You. You are the
Creator and sovereign God. And we give the
glory and the thanksgiving to You, God,
for the ultimate victory that You have promised
Your faithful children.
Amen

☆
54
☆

11

America prays…
with Praise for
the Creator

I will thank you, Lord, in front of all
the people. I will sing your praises among
the nations. For your unfailing love is higher
than the heavens. Your faithfulness
reaches to the clouds.

Psalm 108:3-4 NLT

When we honor God and place Him at the center of our lives, every day is a cause for celebration. God fills each day to the brim with possibilities, and He challenges us to use our lives for His purposes. Every morning, the sun rises over a land of freedom and opportunity.

The new day is presented to us free of charge, but we must beware: Today is a non-renewable resource—once it's gone, it's gone forever. Our responsibility—both as Americans and believers—is to use this day in the service of God's will and in the service of His people.

Today, let us praise God for His blessings, and let us show our gratitude not only through our prayers, but, more importantly, through our deeds.

☆
56
☆

Praise Him! Praise Him!
Tell of His excellent greatness.
Praise Him! Praise Him!
Ever in joyful song!
Fanny Crosby

How delightful a teacher, but gentle
a provider, how bountiful a giver is my Father!
Praise, praise to Thee,
O manifested Most High.
Jim Elliot

☆
57
☆

Praise reestablishes the proper chain of
command; we recognize that the King is on
the throne and that He has saved his people.
Max Lucado

Praise and thank God for who He is and
for what He has done for you.
Billy Graham

A Prayer for America

Lord, Your hand created the smallest grain of
sand and the grandest stars in the heavens.
You watch over Your entire creation, and
You watch over me. Thank You, Lord, for
loving this world so much that You sent Your
Son to die for our sins. Let me always be
grateful for the priceless gift of Your Son,
and let me praise Your holy name forever.
Amen

☆
58
☆

12

America prays…
for Deliverance
from Evil

Even when I walk through the dark valley
of death, I will not be afraid, for you
are close beside me. Your rod and your staff
protect and comfort me.

Psalm 23:4 NLT

Peter offered a stern warning to his Christian brethren: "Your adversary, the devil, prowls around like a roaring lion, seeking someone to devour" (I Peter 5:8 NASB). What was true in New Testament times is equally true in our own. Satan tempts his prey and then seeks to devour them.

As believers, we must beware, and as Americans, we must be vigilant. Evil is indeed abroad in the world, and Satan continues to sow the seeds of destruction far and wide. If we seek righteousness in our own lives *and* in the collective life of our nation, we must earnestly wrap ourselves in the protection of God's Holy Word. When we do, we are secure.

☆
60
☆

The only thing necessary for the triumph
of evil is for good men to do nothing.
Edmund Burke

The world is a dangerous place to live,
not because of the people who are evil,
but because of the people who
don't do anything about it.
Albert Einstein

☆
61
☆

There are a thousand hacking at the branches
of evil to one who is striking at the root.
Henry David Thoreau

We are in a continual battle with the spiritual
forces of evil, but we will triumph when we
yield to God's leading and call on
His powerful presence in prayer.
Shirley Dobson

A Prayer for America

Dear Lord, strengthen my walk with You.
Evil can devour me, and it comes in so many
disguises. Sometimes, Father, I need Your help
to recognize right from wrong. Your presence
in my life enables me to choose truth and
to live a life that is pleasing to You.
May I always live in Your presence, and
may I walk with You today . . . and forever.
Amen

☆
62
☆

13

America prays…
As We Trust in God

It is better to trust the LORD than to put
confidence in people. It is better to trust
the LORD than to put confidence in princes.
Psalm 118:8-9 NLT

Do you seek God's blessings for America? Then pray for our nation. Pray that we the people trust God and follow His Word. If we do, we will continue to receive the blessings that God has so richly bestowed upon us and upon our nation.

Do you seek God's blessings for yourself and your family? Then trust Him. Trust Him with every aspect of your life. Trust Him with your relationships. Trust Him with your finances. Follow His commandments and pray for His guidance. Then, wait patiently for God's revelations and for His blessings. In His own fashion and in His own time, God will bless you in ways that you never could have imagined.

☆
64
☆

Trust the past to God's mercy, the present to God's love, and the future to God's providence.
St. Augustine

Trust in yourself and you are doomed to disappointment; trust in money and you may have it taken from you, but trust in God, and you are never to be confounded in time or eternity.
D. L. Moody

☆
65
☆

That we may not complain of what is, let us see God's hand in all events; and, that we may not be afraid of what shall be, let us see all events in God's hand.
Matthew Henry

Then conquer we must, for our cause is just, and this be our motto: "In God is our Trust!"
Francis Scott Key

A Prayer for America

Dear Lord, when I trust in things of this earth,
I will be disappointed. But, when I put my
faith in You, I am secure. You are my rock and
my shield. Upon Your firm foundation I will
build my life. When I am worried, Lord,
let me trust in You. You will love me and
protect me, and You will share Your boundless
grace today, tomorrow, and forever.
Amen

☆
66
☆

14

America prays...
for the Will
to Persevere

For you have need of endurance,
so that after you have done the will of God,
you may receive the promise.

Hebrews 10:36 NKJV

We know that the key to success, both as individuals and as a nation, is often nothing more than a willingness to persevere. But sometimes, when the storm clouds form overhead and we find ourselves in the dark valley of despair, our faith is stretched to the breaking point. Thankfully, we can always turn to God for comfort: Wherever we find ourselves, whether at the top of the mountain or the depths of the valley, God is there, and because He cares for us, we can live courageously.

The next time you find your courage tested to the limit, remember that God is as near as your next breath, and remember that He offers strength and comfort to His children. He is your shield and your strength; He is your protector and your deliverer. Call upon Him in your hour of need and then be comforted. Whatever your challenge, whatever your trouble, God can help you persevere. And will.

When you get into a tight place and everything
goes against you, till it seems as though you
could not hang on a minute longer,
never give up then, for that is just the place
and the time the tide will turn.

Harriet Beecher Stowe

Stand still and refuse to retreat.
Look at it as God looks at it and draw upon
His power to hold up under the blast.

Chuck Swindoll

☆
69
☆

In the Bible, patience is not a passive
acceptance of circumstances. It is
a courageous perseverance in the face of
suffering and difficulty.

Warren Wiersbe

When we do our best, we never know
what miracles await.

Helen Keller

A Prayer for America

Dear Lord, when the pace of my life
becomes frantic, slow me down and give me
perspective. And Father, when the pace of
world events spins ever faster, keep America's
leaders steady and sure. Give them courage,
perseverance, and wisdom so that, as a nation,
we Americans might remain one nation,
under God . . . forever.
Amen

☆
70
☆

15

America prays...
with Thankful Hearts

Rejoice always, pray without ceasing,
in everything give thanks; for this is
the will of God in Christ Jesus for you.
1 Thessalonians 5:16-18 NKJV

The United States of America is a land of remarkable freedoms and opportunities. Yet as busy citizens living in a demanding world, we may sometimes neglect to thank our Heavenly Father for our nation *and* for the countless *other* blessings that He has seen fit to bestow upon us.

Do you pause many times each day to thank your Creator for His priceless gifts? You should. When you slow down and express your gratitude to the Giver of all things good, you will enrich your own life *and* the lives of those around you. So today and every day, make thanksgiving a habit; make praise a regular part of your daily routine. God has blessed you beyond measure, and you owe Him everything, including your heartfelt thanks.

☆
72
☆

A child of God should be a visible beatitude
for joy and a living doxology for gratitude.
C. H. Spurgeon

The unthankful heart discovers no mercies,
but the thankful heart finds, in every hour,
some heavenly blessings.
Henry Ward Beecher

☆
73
☆

The best way to show my gratitude
to God is to accept everything,
even my problems, with joy.
Mother Teresa

It is only with gratitude that life becomes rich.
Dietrich Bonhoeffer

A Prayer for America

Dear Lord, Your gifts are greater than
I can imagine. May I live each day with
thanksgiving in my heart and praise on my
lips. Thank You for the gift of Your Son and
for the promise of eternal life. Let me share
the joyous news of Jesus Christ, and let my life
be a testimony to His love and to His grace.
Amen

☆
74
☆

16

America prays…
with Hope in
Our Hearts

But happy are those . . . whose hope
is in the LORD their God.

Psalm 146:5 NLT

This world can be a place of trials and tribulations, but as believers we are secure. We need never lose hope because God has promised us peace, joy, and eternal life.

Today's generation of Americans faces challenges and dangers that are unique to this time in world history. But, one thing remains unchanged: we still need our Heavenly Father.

Today, let us pray for faith and courage. Let us live out this day—and every one thereafter—with an unwavering trust in God. When we do, we will be made whole.

☆
76
☆

The essence of optimism is that it takes no account of the present, but it is a source of inspiration, of vitality, and hope where others have resigned; it enables a man to hold his head high, to claim the future for himself, and not to abandon it to his enemy.
Dietrich Bonhoeffer

Great hopes make great men.
Thomas Fuller

☆
77
☆

Hope! What a wonderful word it is! Write it indelibly on your mind. H-O-P-E. It is a bright word, shining and scintillating and dynamic, forward looking, full of courage and optimism. With this word, let us begin tomorrow.
Norman Vincent Peale

Be hopeful! For tomorrow has never happened before.
Robert Schuller

A Prayer for America

Today, Lord, I will trust Your will for my life,
for my family, and for my nation. If I become
discouraged, I will turn to You. If I grow weary,
I will seek strength in You. And,
may the leaders of America also turn to You,
dear God, in these turbulent times.
You are our God and our salvation;
let us place our hopes and our faith in You.
Amen

☆
78
☆

17

America prays...
for Our Families

...these should learn first of all to put
their religion into practice by caring
for their own family...
1 Timothy 5:4 NIV

Are you concerned for the well-being of your family? You are not alone. We live in a world where temptation and danger seem to lurk on every street corner. Parents and children alike have good reason to be watchful. But, despite the evils of our time, God remains steadfast.

These are difficult days for our nation and for our families. But, thankfully, God is bigger than all our challenges. God loves us and protects us. In times of trouble, He comforts us; in times of sorrow, He dries our tears. When we are discouraged, or weak, or sorrowful, God is as near as our next breath.

Let us build our lives *and* our families on the rock that cannot be shaken...let us trust in our Creator. And let us remember that no problems are too big for God. Not even ours.

☆
80
☆

A family is the first and essential cell
of human society.
Pope John XXIII

Whatever the times, one thing
will never change: If you have children,
they must come first. Your success as a family
and our success as a society depends not on
what happens in the White House, but
on what happens inside your house.
Barbara Bush

☆
81
☆

The only true source of meaning in life is
found in love for God and His Son,
Jesus Christ, and love for mankind,
beginning with our own families.
James Dobson

The Golden Rule begins at home.
Marie T. Freeman

A Prayer for America

Dear Lord, I am blessed to be part of
the family of God where I find love and
acceptance. You have also blessed me with
my earthly family. Today I pray for them and
for all the families in America and for families
throughout our world. Protect us and guide us,
Lord. And, as I reach out to my own family,
may I show them the same love and care that
You have shown to me.
Amen

☆
82
☆

18

America prays…
for Wisdom

Reverence for the Lord is the foundation
of true wisdom. The rewards of wisdom
come to all who obey him.

Psalm 111:10 NLT

Sometimes, amid the demands of daily life, we lose perspective. Life seems out of balance, and the pressures of everyday living seem overwhelming. What's needed is a fresh perspective, a restored sense of balance . . . and God's wisdom.

Wisdom results from countless hours spent in heartfelt prayer. It is forged on the anvil of honorable work and polished by the twin virtues of generosity and humility. Wisdom is a priceless thing, and in today's fast changing world, America needs it desperately.

☆
84
☆

Perspective, too, is a precious commodity, one that is often in short supply, especially during difficult days. Today, let us pray for our leaders, that they might possess the insight and the judgment to direct our nation during this time of adversity and change. And, may God grant us, this generation of American citizens, the collective wisdom to select our leaders wisely and the courage to protect our freedoms vigorously.

The years have much to teach
which the days never know.
Ralph Waldo Emerson

Don't expect wisdom to come into your life
like great chunks of rock on a conveyor belt.
Wisdom comes privately from God as a
byproduct of right decisions, godly reactions,
and the application of spiritual principles to
daily circumstances.
Chuck Swindoll

☆
85
☆

If you lack knowledge, go to school.
If you lack wisdom, get on your knees.
Vance Havner

Earthly fears are no fears at all.
Answer the big question of eternity, and
the little questions of life fall into perspective.
Max Lucado

A Prayer for America

Heavenly Father, sometimes, amid the trials of the moment, even the wisest men and women may lose perspective. Today I pray for America's leaders. Give them divine guidance, and lead them according to Your will. And, keep all our citizens mindful that Your reality is the ultimate reality, and that Your wisdom is the ultimate wisdom, now and forever.
Amen

☆
86
☆

19

America prays…
for Justice

The LORD has already told you what is good,
and this is what he requires:
to do what is right, to love mercy,
and to walk humbly with your God.

Micah 6:8 NLT

"With liberty and justice for all." These familiar words from the Pledge of Allegiance remind us that the promise of America is the promise of freedom. And as loyal citizens, we must seek justice not only for ourselves but also for our fellow citizens *and* for those around the world.

America remains a nation dedicated to the principal of equal justice for all its citizens. May we, as modern-day patriots, commit ourselves to lives characterized by truth and justice. And, let us pray that America remains a land of liberty for all of her people.

☆
88
☆

Justice, sir, is the great interest of man on earth. It is the ligament which holds civilized beings and civilized nations together.
Daniel Webster

Standing for right when it is unpopular is a true test of moral character.
Margaret Chase Smith

☆
89
☆

The answer to injustice is not to silence the critic but to end the injustice.
Paul Robeson

Man's capacity for justice makes democracy possible, but man's inclination to injustice makes democracy necessary.
Reinhold Neibuhr

A Prayer for America

☆
90
☆

Dear Lord, You have commanded us to walk humbly and to act justly. Help me to be just in all my personal dealings, and help me, in some small way, to seek justice for all mankind.

Amen

20

America prays...
for Unity

Every kingdom divided against itself will be
ruined, and every city or household divided
against itself will not stand.
Matthew 12:25 NIV

"One nation, under God, indivisible, with liberty and justice for all." We have heard these words on countless occasions, and yet, amid the din of partisanship, we sometimes forget that if America is to remain strong, we, her citizens, must remain united.

We should never confuse unity with unanimity. As men and women of good faith, Americans inevitably disagree about matters of policy. But, we must never allow our differences of opinion to obscure the fact that ours is a great nation precisely *because* of our disagreements. We are a diverse nation composed of independently minded citizens who, because of our collective liberties, are free to think and speak as we see fit. Thankfully, we can do so without fear.

Amid the inevitable disagreements that are part of the grand American debate, we must never sacrifice our unity of purpose: the sincere desire to leave a better nation to the next generation than the one we received from the last. Today, let us pray for America that she might remain free, united, and strong.

Peace without justice is tyranny.
William Allen White

Let it be borne on the flag under which
we rally in every exigency, that we have one
country, one constitution, one destiny.
Daniel Webster

☆
93
☆

No man is above the law, and no man
is below it; nor do we ask any man's
permission when we ask him to obey it.
Theodore Roosevelt

The government is the strongest of
which every man feels himself a part.
Thomas Jefferson

A Prayer for America

Dear Lord, so much more can be accomplished
when we join together to fulfill our common
goals and desires. As I seek to fulfill
Your will for my life, let me also join with
others to accomplish Your greater good for
our nation and for all humanity.
Amen

☆
94
☆

21

America prays...
for Understanding and Tolerance

Now we see but a poor reflection as in a
mirror; then we shall see face to face.
Now I know in part; then I shall know fully,
even as I am fully known.
1 Corinthians 13:12 NIV

Jesus issued a stern warning to Christians of every generation: "Do not judge, and you will not be judged. Do not condemn, and you will not be condemned. Forgive, and you will be forgiven" (Luke 6:37-38 NIV). And yet, because we are fallible human beings, we are often quick to judge others. The irony of our judgments, of course, is that we, too, have fallen short of God's commandments, and we often seek pardon for ourselves (even if we fail to grant it to others).

☆
96
☆

America is a land of tolerance; we Americans are a forgiving people. May it always be so. As Christian believers, we are warned that to judge others is to invite fearful consequences: to the extent we judge others, so, too, will we be judged by God. Let us refrain, then, from judging our neighbors; let us seek, instead to understand them and, when necessary, let us be quick to forgive them—just as God has already forgiven us.

Judging from the main portions of
the history of the world, so far,
justice is always in jeopardy.
Walt Whitman

I hope ever to see America among the foremost
nations in examples of justice and tolerance.
George Washington

No loss by flood and lightning, no destruction
of cities and temples by the hostile forces
of nature, has deprived man of so many noble
lives and impulses as those which
intolerance has destroyed.
Helen Keller

☆
97
☆

If you seek to teach your countrymen
tolerance, you yourself must be tolerant;
if you would teach them liberality for
the opinions of others, you yourself must be
liberal; and if you would teach them
unselfish patriotism, you yourself
must be unselfish and patriotic.
Grover Cleveland

A Prayer for America

Dear Lord, sometimes I am quick to judge
others. But, You have commanded me not to
judge. Keep me mindful, Father, that when
I judge others, I am living outside of Your will
for my life. You have forgiven me, Lord.
Let me forgive others, let me love them, and
let me help them . . . without judging them.
Amen

☆
98
☆

America prays...
for Forgiving Hearts

If you forgive those who sin against you,
your heavenly Father will forgive you.
But if you refuse to forgive others,
your Father will not forgive your sins.
Matthew 6:14-15 NLT

Forgiveness is God's commandment, but oh how difficult a commandment it can be to follow. Being frail, fallible, imperfect human beings, we are quick to anger, quick to blame, slow to forgive, and even slower to forget. No matter. Forgiveness is God's way, and it must be our way, too.

God's Holy Word is a book that must be taken in its entirety; all of God's commandments are to be taken seriously. And, so it is with forgiveness.

☆
100
☆

If, in your heart, you hold bitterness against even a single person, forgive. If there exists even one person, alive or dead, whom you have not forgiven, follow God's commandment and His will for your life: forgive. If you are embittered against yourself for some past mistake or shortcoming, forgive. Then, to the best of your abilities, forget. And move on. For individual citizens *and* for great nations like America, the time to forgive is now.

Develop and maintain the capacity to forgive.
Martin Luther King, Jr.

When God tells us to love our enemies,
He gives, along with the command,
the love itself.
Corrie ten Boom

☆
101
☆

There is no revenge so complete
as forgiveness.
Josh Billings

Forgiveness is the final form of love.
Reinhold Niebuhr

A Prayer for America

Dear Lord, when I am bitter, You can change
my unforgiving heart. Let me be Your obedient
servant, Lord, and let me forgive others just
as You have forgiven me. And Father,
give the leaders of our nation a spirit
of forgiveness and reconciliation so that
America might be an instrument of
Your will here on earth.
Amen

☆
102
☆

23

America prays…
for a Spirit of
Generosity

Freely you have received, freely give.
Matthew 10:8 NIV

God's Word instructs us that service to others is one way of fulfilling His purpose here on earth. Romans 12:10 reminds us, "Be devoted to one another in brotherly love" (NIV). Thankfully, Americans of every generation have heeded these words.

☆
104
☆

We live in a world in which too many people must struggle to obtain the basic necessities of life. As Americans, we have been richly blessed, and we must be quick to share our blessings. Whether the needs are here at home or far away, the response is the same: we, as responsible citizens of the most prosperous nation on earth, must care enough to help.

Give what you have. To someone,
it may be better than you dare to think.
Henry Wadsworth Longfellow

The mind grows by taking in,
but the heart grows by giving out.
Warren Wiersbe

☆
105
☆

He climbs the highest who helps another up.
Zig Ziglar

What is serving God? 'Tis doing good to man.
Poor Richard's Almanac

A Prayer for America

Dear Lord, Your gifts are beyond
comprehension. You gave Your Son, Jesus,
to save us, and Your motivation was love.
I pray that the gifts I give to others will come
from an overflow of my heart, and that they
will echo the great love You have for
all of Your children.
Amen

☆
106
☆

24

America prays...
for the Freedoms
We Hold Dear

Where the Spirit of the Lord is,
there is freedom.
2 Corinthians 3:17 NIV

Perhaps you have sometimes taken America's freedoms for granted. If so, welcome to the club. In a land so richly blessed, it is easy to forget how hard our forefathers struggled to earn the blessings that we enjoy today. But, we must never forget, and we must never become complacent.

Abraham Lincoln's words still ring true: "No man is good enough to govern another man without the other's consent." But, across the globe, tyranny and oppression still grip the lives of far too many innocent men, women, and children. When people anywhere are denied their freedoms, people everywhere are threatened. And so it is that American men and women must, on occasion, travel far beyond our borders to protect the lives and liberties of foreign citizens.

In America, no man governs alone. We the people make the laws, enforce the laws, and change the laws when those laws need changing. For these liberties, we must thank those who have gone before us *and* our Father who reins above us. And, the best way to say "thank you" for our blessings is to defend them, whatever the cost.

☆
108
☆

Resistance to tyrants is obedience to God.
Ben Franklin

Freedom is the last, best hope of earth.
Abraham Lincoln

Everything that is really good and
inspiring is created by individuals
who labor in freedom.
Albert Einstein

☆
109
☆

If it be the pleasure of Heaven that my country
shall require the poor offering of my life,
the victim shall be ready, at the appointed
hour of sacrifice, come when that hour may.
But while I do live, let me have
a country that is free.
John Adams

A Prayer for America

Thank You, Dear Lord, for this nation
and for the freedoms we enjoy here. Give us
the courage to preserve our precious liberties
and the strength to share them with oppressed
people around the world. May we speak out
against injustice and oppression of any
kind...anywhere. And, may the flame of
freedom that burns brightly here in America
be a beacon for all the world to see.
Amen

☆
110
☆

25

America prays…
for Our Children

Train up a child in the way he should go, and
when he is old he will not depart from it.
Proverbs 22:6 NKJV

Our children are this nation's most precious resource. And, as responsible adults, we must create a homeland in which the next generation of Americans can live in safety and in freedom. Thankfully, the American Dream is alive and well; it is our responsibility to ensure that it remains so. We must protect our nation's liberties with the same sense of dedication and urgency that our forebears demonstrated when they earned those liberties on the fields of battle and in the halls of justice.

Today, let us pray for our children ... *all* of them. Let us pray for children here at home *and* for children around the world. Every child is God's child. May we, as concerned adults, behave—and pray— accordingly.

☆
112
☆

Children are the hands by which
we take hold of heaven.
Henry Ward Beecher

Praying for our children is a noble task.
There is nothing more special, more precious,
than time that a parent spends struggling and
pondering with God on behalf of a child.
Max Lucado

☆
113
☆

Let's please God by actively seeking,
through prayer, "peaceful and quiet lives"
for ourselves, our spouses, our children and
grandchildren, our friends, and our nation.
Shirley Dobson

Every child born into the world is
a new thought of God, an ever-fresh
and radiant possibility.
Kate Douglas Wiggin

A Prayer for America

Lord, the children of this world are
Your children. Let us love them,
care for them, nurture them, teach them,
and lead them to You. And today,
as I serve as an example to the children
under my care, let my words and deeds
demonstrate the love that I feel
for them . . . and for You.
Amen

☆
114
☆

26

America prays…
for Patience

Wait patiently on the Lord.
Be brave and courageous.
Yes, wait patiently on the Lord.
Psalm 27:14 NLT

As individuals and as a nation, we become impatient for the changes that we so earnestly desire. We want solutions to our problems, and we want them now! But sometimes, life's greatest challenges defy easy solutions, so we must be patient.

☆
116
☆

Psalm 27:14 commands us to wait patiently for God, but, for most of us, waiting quietly for Him is difficult. Why? Because we are fallible human beings who desire solutions to our problems today, if not sooner. We seek to manage our lives according to our own timetables, not God's. Still, God instructs us to be patient in all things, and that is as it should be. After all, think how patient God has been with us.

Genius is nothing more than
a greater aptitude for patience.
Ben Franklin

All good abides with him who waits wisely.
Henry David Thoreau

Waiting means going about our assigned tasks,
confident that God will provide
the meaning and the conclusions.
Eugene Peterson

The next time you're disappointed,
don't panic and don't give up. Just be patient
and let God remind you He's still in control.
Max Lucado

A Prayer for America

Dear Lord, make our nation a land of wisdom,
patience, and perseverance . . . starting
with me. May I live according to Your plan
and according to Your timetable. When
I am hurried, slow me down. When I become
impatient with others, give me empathy. Today,
let me be a patient servant as I trust in You,
Father, and in Your master plan.

Amen

☆
118
☆

27

America prays...
for Those Who Long to Breathe Free

The Spirit of the Lord is on me, because he has
anointed me to preach good news to the poor.
He has sent me to proclaim freedom for the
prisoners and recovery of sight for the blind,
to release the oppressed, to proclaim
the year of the Lord's favor.

Luke 4:18-19 NIV

As citizens of America, many of us have enjoyed our liberties for so long that sometimes we take them for granted. Others do not. All around the globe, hardworking men and women long to come to our shores and breathe the fresh air of freedom. While our nation cannot welcome all people who wish to make America their home, we *can* do our part to spread the gospel of freedom and justice throughout the world . . . and we should.

In his second letter to the church in Corinth, Paul writes, "Where the Spirit of the Lord is, there is freedom" (3:17 NIV). Today, let us pray for those people around the world who seek freedom, and let us do whatever we can to help them find it.

☆
120
☆

The aspiration toward freedom is the most
essentially human of all human manifestations.
Eric Hoffer

America means opportunity, freedom, power.
Ralph Waldo Emerson

The bosom of America is open to receive not
only the opulent and respectable stranger, but
the oppressed and persecuted of all Nations
and religions, whom we shall welcome in
participation of all our rights and privileges,
if by decency and propriety of conduct they
appear to merit the enjoyment.
George Washington

☆
121
☆

Sell all and purchase liberty.
Patrick Henry

A Prayer for America

Dear Lord, You have blessed me with
the opportunity to live in a nation that
treasures freedom. I know that some people
in this world are not as fortunate. Today,
I pray for all humanity, especially those
who long to breathe free. May they find
the liberties that they so earnestly seek,
and may they live their lives in peace,
security, and happiness.
Amen

☆
122
☆

28

America prays…
to Know God's Will
and His Word

Your word is a lamp to my feet
and a light for my path.
Psalm 119:105 NIV

These are difficult days for America. We are faced with challenges—both from inside our borders and from outside them—that are new to this generation. In difficult times such as these, we learn lessons that we could have learned in no other way: We learn about life, but more importantly, we learn about ourselves.

Adversity visits us all. But, Old Man Trouble is not only an unwelcome guest, he is also an invaluable teacher. If we are to become mature human beings, it is our duty to learn from the inevitable hardships and heartbreaks of life.

When we trust God completely, we have every reason to live courageously. God is in His heaven, we are His children, and He is in control. May we follow His Word and seek His will, knowing that faith in the Father is the immovable cornerstone in the foundation of courageous living.

The Bible is the Rock on which
this Republic rests.
Andrew Jackson

All the good from the Savior of the world is
communicated through this Book, the Bible;
but for the Book we could not know right
from wrong. All the things desirable
to man are contained in it.
Abraham Lincoln

☆
125
☆

It is impossible to rightly govern the world
without God and the Bible. Do not ever let
anyone claim to be a true American patriot
if they ever attempt to separate
Religion from politics.
George Washington

The Bible is like no other book.
Treat it that way!
Marie T. Freeman

A Prayer for America

As I journey through this life, Lord,
help me always to consult the true road map:
Your Holy Word. I know that when I turn my
heart and my thoughts to You, Father,
You will lead me along the path that is right
for me. And, when our nation's leaders seek
Your will, they, too, will discover the wisdom
of Your Holy Word. Today, dear Lord,
let me know Your will and study Your Word,
and let America's leaders fulfill
Your plan for our nation.
Amen

☆
126
☆

29

America prays…
for Renewal and Strength

Those who hope in the LORD will renew their
strength. They will soar on wings like eagles;
they will run and not grow weary,
they will walk and not be faint.

Isaiah 40:31 NIV

For many Americans, these are difficult days indeed. Adversity, of course, visits everyone in time—no one is exempt. And, when difficult times arrive, we may become discouraged or worse. Thankfully, there is a source from which we can draw the power needed to renew our strength. That source is God.

God intends that His children lead joyous lives filled with abundance and peace. But sometimes, abundance and peace seem very far away. It is then that we must turn to God for renewal, and when we do, He will restore us.

Are you tired or troubled? Turn your heart toward God in prayer. Are you weak or worried? Take the time to delve deeply into God's Holy Word. Are you spiritually depleted? Call upon fellow believers to support you, and call upon God to renew your spirit and your life. When you do, you'll discover that the Creator of the universe stands always ready and always able to create a new sense of wonderment and joy in you.

☆

128

☆

Sometimes, we need a housecleaning
of the heart.
Catherine Marshall

God is not running an antique shop!
He is making all things new!
Vance Havner

Prayer plumes the wings of God's young
eaglets so that they may learn to mount above
the clouds. Prayer brings inner strength
to God's warriors and sends them forth
to spiritual battle with their muscles firm
and their armor in place.
C. H. Spurgeon

☆
129
☆

Do not pray for easy lives.
Pray to be stronger men!
Do not pray for tasks equal to your powers.
Pray for powers equal to your tasks.
Phillips Brooks

A Prayer for America

Heavenly Father, sometimes I am troubled,
and sometimes I grow weary. When I am weak,
Lord, give me strength. When I am
discouraged, renew me. When I am fearful,
let me feel Your healing touch. Let me always
trust in Your promises, Lord, and let me draw
strength from those promises
and from Your unending love.
Amen

☆
130
☆

30

America prays…
for God's Grace

My grace is sufficient for you,
for my power is made perfect in weakness.
2 Corinthians 12:9 NIV

None of us have earned the freedoms and opportunities that we enjoy here in America; those blessings are a cumulative bequest of our forebears and a priceless gift from God above. Today, let us pray that God continues to bless this nation, and that His grace will touch the hearts of all our people.

☆
132
☆

Let us praise God for His gifts, and let us share His Word with all who cross our paths. God's grace is the ultimate gift, and we owe to Him the ultimate in thanksgiving. We demonstrate our thanks by sharing His message and His love.

Yes, God's grace is always sufficient,
and His arms are always open to give it.
But, will our arms be open to receive it?
Beth Moore

God shares Himself generously and graciously.
Eugene Peterson

☆
133
☆

Grace: a gift that costs everything for
the giver and nothing for the recipient.
Philip Yancey

God does amazing works through prayers
that seek to extend His grace to others.
Shirley Dobson

A Prayer for America

Dear God, Your grace is a priceless gift to
Your children. We thank You, Lord,
and praise You for Your blessings. We ask
that You continue to bless America. Lead
this nation, Father, according to Your will
so that we might be worthy of Your gifts.
Amen

☆
134
☆

31

America prays...
for Our World

Confess your trespasses to one another, and
pray for one another, that you may be healed.
The effective, fervent prayer of
a righteous man avails much.

James 5:16 NKJV

This world can be a dangerous place. But, as believers, we are comforted by the knowledge that God still sits in His heaven. He sees the grand scope of His creation, a vision that we, as mortals, cannot see.

Even though we never fully understand God's plan, we must trust His wisdom and His will, and we must seek to do His will here on earth.

☆
136
☆

Today, we pray for the world, that it might finally become a place of peace and freedom for all God's children. We petition God for His blessings on our generation, and we seek to live according to His commandments as we do His work and share His love.

We have staked the future of American
civilization upon the capacity of each and
all of us to govern ourselves according to
the Ten Commandments of God.
James Madison

Turning our eyes to other nations, our great
desire is to see our brethren of the human race
secured in the blessings enjoyed by ourselves,
and advancing in knowledge, in freedom,
and in social happiness.
Andrew Jackson

☆
137
☆

Real power in prayer flows only when
a man's spirit touches God's spirit.
Catherine Marshall

History has been changed time after time
because of prayer. I tell you, history could be
changed again if people went to their knees
in believing prayer.
Billy Graham

A Prayer for America

Dear Lord, today I pray for this world and
the people who inhabit it. Make me Your
prayer warrior, a person who is concerned not
only for the circumstances of my own life but
also for the entirety of your earthly creation.
Let me make my contribution, however small,
to ensure that Your will is done here
on earth, just as it is in heaven.
Amen

☆
138
☆

Bible Verses by Topic

Courage

The LORD is my light and my salvation;
whom shall I fear? The LORD is the strength
of my life; of whom shall I be afraid?
Psalm 27:1 KJV

☆
140
☆

Be on guard. Stand true to what you believe.
Be courageous. Be strong.
1 Corinthians 16:13 NLT

Be of good courage, And He shall strengthen
your heart, All you who hope in the LORD.
Psalm 31:24 NKJV

Do not be afraid
or discouraged.
For the LORD
your God is with you
wherever you go.

—

Joshua 1:9 NLT

☆
141
☆

Faith

But he must ask in faith without any doubting,
for the one who doubts is like the surf
of the sea, driven and tossed by the wind.
James 1:6 NASB

☆
142
☆

Be on the alert, stand firm in the faith,
act like men, be strong.
1 Corinthians 16:13 NASB

For the LORD watches over
the way of the righteous, but
the way of the wicked will perish.
Psalm 1:6 NIV

If you do not stand firm
in your faith,
you will not stand at all.

—

Isaiah 7:9 NIV

☆
143
☆

God's Love

For God so loved the world that he gave his
one and only Son, that whoever believes in
him shall not perish but have eternal life.
John 3:16 NIV

☆
144
☆

The unfailing love of the LORD never ends!
Lamentations 3:22 NLT

We know how much God loves us,
and we have put our trust in him.
God is love, and all who live in love
live in God, and God lives in them.
1 John 4:16 NLT

Unfailing love surrounds
those who trust the LORD.

—

Psalm 32:10 NLT

☆
145
☆

Renewal

I will give you a new heart
and put a new spirit in you....
Ezekiel 36:26 NIV

☆
146
☆

He makes me to lie down in green pastures;
He leads me beside the still waters.
He restores my soul;
He leads me in the paths of righteousness
For His name's sake.
Psalm 23:2–3 NKJV

Create in me a clean heart, O God;
and renew a right spirit within me.
Psalm 51:10 KJV

He restoreth my soul.

—

Psalm 23:3 KJV

☆
147
☆

Encouraging Others

Take heed, brethren, lest there be
in any of you an evil heart of unbelief,
in departing from the living God. But exhort
one another daily, while it is called Today;
lest any of you be hardened through
the deceitfulness of sin.
Hebrews 3:12-13 KJV

☆
148
☆

Let us consider how to stimulate
one another to love and good deeds.
Hebrews 10:24 KJV

Do not let any unwholesome talk come out
of your mouths, but only what is helpful for
building others up according to their needs,
that it may benefit those who listen.
Ephesians 4:29 NIV

So then we pursue the things which make for peace and the building up of one another.

—

Romans 14:19 NASB

☆
149
☆

Peace

Peace I leave with you, My peace I give to
you; not as the world gives do I give to you.
Let not your heart be troubled.
John 14:27 NKJV

☆

150

☆

Those who love Your law have great peace,
and nothing causes them to stumble.
Psalm 119:165 NASB

If it is possible, as far as it depends on you,
live at peace with everyone.
Romans 12:18 NIV

And the seed whose fruit is
righteousness is sown in peace
by those who make peace.

—

James 3:18 NASB

☆
151
☆

Forgiving Others

A man's wisdom gives him patience;
it is to his glory to overlook an offense.
Proverbs 19:11 NIV

☆
152
☆

Blessed are the merciful:
for they shall obtain mercy.
Matthew 5:7 KJV

Then came Peter to him, and said, Lord,
how oft shall my brother sin against me, and
I forgive him? till seven times? Jesus saith
unto him, I say not unto thee, Until seven
times: but, Until seventy times seven.
Matthew 18:21-22 KJV

Be kind to one another,
tender-hearted, forgiving
each other, just as God
in Christ also has forgiven
you.

—

Ephesians 4:32 NASB

☆
153
☆

Prayer

Rejoice evermore. Pray without ceasing.
In every thing give thanks: for this is the will
of God in Christ Jesus concerning you.
1 Thessalonians 5:16-18 KJV

☆
154
☆

Be joyful in hope, patient in affliction,
faithful in prayer.
Romans 12:12 NIV

Be anxious for nothing, but in everything by
prayer and supplication, with thanksgiving,
let your requests be made known to God.
Philippians 4:6 NKJV

Confess your trespasses to one another, and pray for one another, that you may be healed. The effective, fervent prayer of a righteous man avails much.

—

James 5:16 NKJV

☆
155
☆